Freestyle Motocross

Rev It Up!

Jackie Golusky

Lerner Publications ◆ Minneapolis

Lerner Publications Company
An imprint of Lerner Publishing Group, Inc.
241 First Avenue North
Minneapolis, MN 55401 USA

For reading levels and more information, look up this title at www.lernerbooks.com.

Main body text set in Billy Infant Regular. Typeface provided by SparkType.

Editor: Lauren Foley

Library of Congress Cataloging-in-Publication Data

Names: Golusky, Jackie, 1996- author.
Title: Freestyle motocross : rev it up! / Jackie Golusky.
Description: Minneapolis : Lerner Publications, 2023. | Series: Lightning bolt books. Dirt bike zone | Includes bibliographical references and index. | Audience: Ages 6–9 | Audience: Grades 2–3 | Summary: "Flip into Freestyle Motocross. Young learners will dive into the exciting world of Freestyle tricks while discovering more about safety gear, competitions, and more"— Provided by publisher.
Identifiers: LCCN 2022014638 (print) | LCCN 2022014639 (ebook) | ISBN 9781728476308 (library binding) | ISBN 9781728478722 (paperback) | ISBN 9781728483184 (ebook)
Subjects: LCSH: Motocross—Juvenile literature.
Classification: LCC GV1060.12 .G65 2023 (print) | LCC GV1060.12 (ebook) | DDC 796.7/56—dc23/eng/20220328

LC record available at https://lccn.loc.gov/2022014638
LC ebook record available at https://lccn.loc.gov/2022014639

Manufactured in the United States of America
1-52211-50651-6/14/2022

Table of Contents

Cool Tricks

A Freestyle Motocross rider races up a dirt hill. As he flies into the air, the rider has a chance to show off his tricks and impress the judges.

The rider swings his legs behind him off the bike while his hands hold the handlebars. He completes a nine o'clock nac. Crowds cheer.

Big Air and Freestyle

Freestyle Motocross, or FMX, is a type of dirt bike racing that focuses on tricks. Riders create new tricks to earn points from the judges and show their creativity.

FMX comes from Motocross. Motocross is another type of dirt bike racing.

A Motocross racer rounds a turn.

FMX riders compete on human-made tracks. Some tracks have special ramps and landings designed to cut down on injuries from falls.

FMX has two types of events: big air and freestyle. Big air is also called best trick. Riders get two jumps to perform tricks. They earn points for difficulty, style, and originality.

A rider performs a trick during a FMX event. Riders earn more points on difficult tricks.

In freestyle, riders perform two routines on a track with jumps. The jumps have different angles and heights. This event lasts between 1.5 and 14 minutes. The judges' score is based on the tricks.

A FMX rider soars over a jump. Freestyle events have many jumps.

Freestyle Bikes and More

Riders can get hurt during tricks, so they wear protective gear. They wear helmets to protect their heads. Goggles prevent dirt from flying into their eyes.

Most FMX riders use a two-stroke or four-stroke dirt bike. Both bikes have similar engines. But a four-stroke bike is less powerful.

Two-stroke bikes are lighter. So some tricks like backflips are easier to do on these bikes. But they need more fuel than four-stroke bikes.

It's easier to do backflips on a lighter dirt bike.

What's Next for FMX?

The biggest FMX stars face off at the X Games and Nitro World Games. At both events, riders race around a course and perform their best tricks. They hope to take home the gold medal.

Many world firsts happen at the Nitro World Games. Ramps and landings are designed so riders can show off their skills.

A Nitro Games rider jumping over a castle

Vicki Golden already had three X Games golds for Motocross when she competed in the X Games Best Whip for FMX. She was the first woman to compete in the event. She won bronze.

Vicki Golden twists in the air during the 2013 X Games Best Whip.

Takayuki (Taka) Higashino has five X Games medals. Three are gold. He was the first rider to land a rock-solid backflip. The rider does a full backflip while letting go of the handlebars.

Luc Ackermann won gold at the 2021 X Games. He scored an amazing 92.33 on his first moto. No one could beat him.

Luc Ackermann grabs the seat to keep the bike still as he performs a trick.

Fans love to watch FMX events and cheer on riders.

Freestyle Motocross riders continue to develop their tricks. They want to keep pushing the boundaries of FMX. Fans can't wait to see what they do next.

Bike Diagram

Kawasaki KX450F

How It Works

How do FMX riders complete tricks on their bikes? They speed up a ramp, which helps them jump into the air. In the air, riders have seconds to complete their trick before landing. Then they need to return to sitting on their bikes with their hands on the handlebars to land safely. FMX bikes are lightweight, so it's easier for them to soar into the air.

Glossary

design: planning how something is built or created

engine: a machine that changes energy into mechanical motion

handlebars: bars with handles for steering a bike

moto: one of several races to decide who will win

Motocross: a type of dirt bike racing where riders compete on a course with obstacles

originality: the quality of being new and different

routine: a series of movements or tricks that are part of a performance

style: a certain way of doing something

Learn More

Ducksters: MotoX Motocross
https://www.ducksters.com/sports/extrememotox.php

Golusky, Jackie. *Motocross: Rev It Up!* Minneapolis: Lerner Publications, 2023.

Hale, K. A. *Freestyle Motocross*. Minnetonka, MN: Kaleidoscope, 2019.

Hudak, Heather C. *Motocross*. New York: AV2, 2021.

Kidz World: Motocross 101
https://www.kidzworld.com/article/6121-motocross-101/

X Games Facts for Kids
https://kids.kiddle.co/X_Games

Index

Photo Acknowledgments

Image credits: AP Photo/Ben Liebenberg, p. 4; Alexander Hassenstein/Bongarts/Getty Images, p. 5; Paul Kane/Getty Images, p. 6; Cameron Spencer/Getty Images, p. 7; Mathias Kniepeiss/Getty Images, p. 8; LIONEL BONAVENTURE/AFP/Getty Images, p. 9; Aref Karimi/AFP/Getty Images, p. 10; Rolf Simeon/Alamy Stock Photo, p. 11; Mondadori Portfolio/Getty Images, p. 12; Dave Etheridge-Barnes/Getty Images, p. 13; Phillip Ellsworth/Getty Images, p. 14; Ben Birchall/PA Images/Getty Images, p. 15; MediaNews Group/Torrance Daily Breeze/Getty Images, p. 16; Mirco Lazzari/Getty Images, p. 17; Michal Krumphanzl/CTK Photo/Alamy Stock Photo, p. 18; Daniel Pockett - CA/Getty Images, p. 19; © Leighton Smith, p. 20.

Cover image: hurricanehank/Shutterstock.